Money Matters

The Big Book of World Currencies

Priyanka Verma

DIAMOND BOOKS

www.diamondbooks.in

Publisher : **Diamond Pocket Books (P) Ltd.**
X-30, Okhla Industrial Area, Phase-II
New Delhi-110020
Phone : 011-40712200
E-mail : wecare@diamondbooks.in
Website : www.diamondbooks.in
Edition : 2025
Printed By : Repro (India)

Preface

Welcome to the exciting journey of money!

From ancient seashells to today's digital wallets, currency has evolved in fascinating ways. This book is designed to help students in Grades 6–8 explore the world of currencies — not just as coins and notes, but as a reflection of culture, history, economics, and innovation.

Aligned with the National Education Policy 2020 and the National Curriculum Framework 2023, this book encourages experiential and competency-based learning. Through activities, real-world connections, and simple storytelling, we aim to build critical thinkers who understand how the global economy connects with their daily lives.

- Priyanka Verma

Foreword

In a world where financial literacy is becoming essential, introducing currency education at the middle-school level is both timely and visionary. This book provides a unique window into the global economic landscape while aligning perfectly with India's NEP 2020 goals. By nurturing curiosity and interdisciplinary thinking, this book helps students explore how history, geography, technology, and culture influence money.

Contents

Chapter 1

What is Money?

The Birth of Currency

Story Starter
Imagine you live in a small village long ago. You grow rice but need a pair of sandals. Your neighbor makes sandals but doesn't want rice—she wants milk. Now you have to find someone who has milk and wants rice. Only then can you trade and get those sandals!

That sounds like a lot of work, right?

Curiosity Question
Why do we use money today instead of just exchanging goods?

Explore

1. What is Money?
Money is anything that people agree can be used to buy and sell goods or services. It could be coins, paper notes, or even something

digital like money in a mobile wallet.

Key Point: Money is not just about buying—it's about making trade simple.

2. Why Was Money Invented?

Before money, people used the barter system. That means they exchanged things—like wheat for a goat or cloth for a basket of mangoes.

But barter had big problems:

- Both people had to want what the other had (called a double coincidence of wants).
- You couldn't divide goods easily (how do you trade half a cow?).
- It was hard to store or carry.

So, humans invented money—a common thing everyone could accept in exchange.

3. Early Forms of Money

Did you know? People once used:

- Cowrie shells in Africa and India
- Salt in ancient Rome (the word "salary" comes from salt!)
- Cattle in tribal societies
- Grain in Egypt
- Metal coins in China, Greece, and India

Illustration idea:

Visual timeline from Barter → Shells → Salt → Metal Coins → Paper Notes → Digital Money

Cartoon-style barter marketplace scene

4. What Makes Something "Money"?

To be accepted as money, an item must be:

- Portable (easy to carry)
- Divisible (can be split into smaller units)
- Durable (won't rot or break)
- Recognized (trusted by everyone)

Try It

Activity 1: Barter Market Role Play
Split into pairs. Each student gets a card (e.g., "3 apples", "1 pair of shoes", "2 kg of rice"). Try to barter for something you need. Can everyone get what they want?

Activity 2: Make Your Own Money
Design your own classroom currency.

Decide:

- What material it's made of
- What symbol or name it has
- Why it's useful

Display your designs on a class board!

Think & Reflect

1. If we didn't have money, how would you get your school books, clothes, or lunch?
2. Do you think digital money like UPI is real money? Why or why not?
3. Can anything become money if people agree to use it?

Let's Revise

Quick Recap:

- Before money, people used barter.
- Barter was difficult, so people invented money to make trade easier.

• Early money included shells, salt, cattle, and coins.
• Good money must be portable, divisible, durable, and widely accepted.

Memory Tip:
Barter is hard, money is smart!

Check Yourself

Multiple Choice Questions

1. What is one major problem with the barter system?
a) Too much money
b) Can't find exact exchange
c) Too many sellers
Answer: b) Can't find exact exchange

2. Which of the following was once used as money?
a) Water
b) Air
c) Salt
Answer: c) Salt

Short Answer
Q: Why did early humans stop using barter?

Creative Question
Imagine your school has its own currency. What would you name it and how would students earn it?

Beyond the Book

Project Suggestion:

Ask your parents or grandparents if they remember old coins or notes. Try to collect photos or drawings of different types of money India has used. Create a scrapbook titled “My Family’s Money Memory”.

Chapter 2

Barter to Bitcoin

How Money Evolved

Real-Life Scenario

Imagine you're shopping online. With a single tap, your parents pay for your schoolbag using a QR code. No cash, no coins—just a few digital numbers.

Now, travel back thousands of years. There's no phone, no card, not even coins! People are trading goats for clothes and rice for pots. So how did we go from that to today?

Curiosity Question

How did money change from goats to Google Pay?

Explore

1. The Beginning: Barter System

In early civilizations, people exchanged goods and services directly—this is called barter.

Example: Rani gives wheat to Meera and gets honey in return.

Problems with Barter:

- Both people had to need what the other had
- No standard value (Is 1 pot equal to 10 bananas?)
- Couldn't save wealth or use later

So, people looked for something better. This led to…

2. Commodity Money

Some items were seen as more useful, rare, or easy to carry:

- Cowrie shells in Africa and Asia
- Salt in Rome
- Cattle in tribal areas
- Metal pieces in China and Mesopotamia

These were called "commodity money" because they had value even outside of trade.

3. Coin Revolution: The Birth of Metal Money

Around 600 BCE, Lydia (in modern Turkey) made the first official coins using gold and silver.

India's own punch-marked coins were made around the same time—small silver pieces stamped with symbols.

Why coins?

- Easy to carry and count
- Durable and long-lasting
- Hard to fake

Illustration Idea:
A side-by-side drawing:
→ A tribal barter scene

→ An ancient Indian trader holding silver punch-marked coins

4. Paper Money Arrives

Paper money began in China during the Tang dynasty (around 7th century CE) and became popular in the Song dynasty.

Later, Europe and the Mughal Empire in India adopted this idea. Paper was easier to print, carry, and store.

5. Banking and Promissory Notes

In India, banias (traditional bankers) used hundis—a kind of written promise to pay money. These were early banking systems!

Fun Fact: The word "bank" comes from the Italian word banco, meaning bench—where early bankers sat!

6. The Era of Plastic and Digital Money

In the 20th century, things moved fast:

- Credit cards (1950s)
- Debit cards
- ATMs
- Online banking

And now?

- Digital wallets like UPI, Google Pay, and PhonePe
- Cryptocurrencies like Bitcoin (introduced in 2009)

Note: Cryptocurrencies are a form of decentralized digital money—not controlled by any government or bank.

7. Why Does Money Keep Changing?

Because the way we live, trade, and communicate changes! As technology improves, we find faster, safer, and more efficient ways to manage money.

Try It

Activity 1: Money Timeline Game

Give students flashcards with these terms:
Barter, Cowrie Shells, Metal Coins, Paper Notes, Credit Cards, UPI, Bitcoin.
Ask them to arrange in order and stick on a "Money Evolution Wall."

Activity 2: Design Your Future Money
What do you think money will look like in 2050? A bracelet that pays? Face-scan currency?
Draw your idea and write one line explaining how it works.

Think & Reflect

1. Why do you think people trusted cowrie shells or gold as money?
2. What is one advantage of digital money? One risk?
3. Will there always be paper money, or will it disappear one day?

Let's Revise

Quick Recap:
- Money started with barter but evolved to suit changing times.
- Early money included commodities like shells, salt, and cattle.
- Coins made trade easier and trustworthy.
- Paper money, credit cards, and now digital money followed.
- Technology and trust shape how we use money.

Remember: From barter to Bitcoin, money reflects human needs and imagination.

Check Yourself

MCQs

1. What was the main problem with the barter system?
a) Too many shops
b) Hard to carry cows
c) No common value

2. Which was the first country to use paper money?
a) India
b) Italy
c) China

Short Answer
Q: What are cryptocurrencies, and how are they different from regular money?

Creative Question
If your school had digital money, how would students earn and spend it?

Beyond the Book

Project Suggestion:
Interview a parent, grandparent, or neighbor. Ask:
- What type of money they used as children?
- When they first saw a credit card or ATM?
- What they think of digital payments today?

Make a "Then vs Now" chart to share in class.

Chapter 3

Ancient Currencies of the World

Story Starter
Imagine you're a young traveler in a time machine. You visit Egypt, China, Rome, and ancient India. In each place, people are buying and selling—but with very different kinds of money. Some use metal coins, others shells, and some even use stones as big as car tires!

Curiosity Question
Why did different civilizations use different types of currency?

Explore

1. What Are Ancient Currencies?
Ancient currencies were the early forms of money used thousands of years ago before modern coins and notes. These currencies show how people in different regions valued different materials and objects.

2. Ancient India – Punch-Marked Coins
India was among the first to mint coins. Around 600 BCE,

Mahajanapadas (ancient kingdoms) used punch-marked silver coins. Each coin had symbols punched onto it like a sun, elephant, or tree.
- Made of silver
- No ruler's image, just symbols
- Used widely in trade

Fun Fact: The word "Rupee" comes from Rupya, meaning silver in Sanskrit!

3. China – The Cowry Shell and Knife Coins
- Cowry shells were used as money as early as 1200 BCE.
- Later, China introduced knife-shaped and spade-shaped bronze coins.
- Eventually, they made round coins with a square hole, which became standard.

Illustration idea:
A hand holding punch-marked coins, Chinese knife coin, and round coin with hole.

4. Mesopotamia – Clay Tablets and Grain
In Sumer (modern Iraq), the earliest traders recorded payments on clay tablets. They often used grain (especially barley) as money.
- Grain was stored in temples
- Payments were measured in baskets

5. Egypt – Grain Banks and Gold Rings
Ancient Egyptians didn't use coins much. **Instead:**
- Grain was the main currency
- Gold rings called Shat were also used in high-value trade
- Temples acted as grain banks

6. Rome – Salt and Metal Coins
In Ancient Rome:
- Roman soldiers were sometimes paid in salt (where the word

salary comes from!)

- Later, they used metal coins made of bronze, silver, and gold
- Roman coins had images of emperors, gods, and battles

Try to Spot: Julius Caesar's face on early Roman coins

7. Africa – Iron Tools and Beads

In parts of Africa:

- People used iron tools like spears, hoes, or knives as money
- Colorful beads and cowries were used for smaller transactions
- These items were valued for both beauty and usefulness

8. Pacific Islands – Rai Stones

In the island of Yap (Micronesia), people used giant stone discs called Rai stones.

- Some were up to 12 feet wide!
- Too big to carry—ownership was passed by word of mouth
- Used for special occasions like marriages or treaties

Illustration idea:

Giant Rai stone next to a hut, with children pointing in awe.

9. American Civilizations – Cocoa Beans and Feathers

- Aztecs used cocoa beans as money!
- Incas used cloth and labor as currency
- Feathers, shells, and colorful stones were also valued

Why Were Ancient Currencies So Different?

Because cultures chose what they valued:

- **Availability:** What was common in their region
- **Belief systems:** Some items were sacred
- **Trade networks:** Some goods were rare and exotic

Money was not just about buying—it was about identity, belief, and value.

Try It

Activity 1: Currency Travel Map

Create a large world map in your classroom. Mark regions and paste pictures of ancient currencies (shells, coins, cocoa beans, etc.). Label them with civilization names.

Activity 2: Ancient Currency Show-and-Tell

Bring a drawing or sample of an ancient currency (real or handmade).

Explain:

- What it was made of
- Why it was used
- What its value might have been

Think & Reflect

1. Why do you think people trusted cowries or stones as money?
2. If you lived in ancient Egypt or China, which currency would you prefer and why?
3. What does a civilization's currency tell us about its lifestyle and trade?

Let's Revise

Quick Recap:

- Ancient currencies were creative and based on local culture.
- India used silver punch-marked coins; China used shells and shaped coins.
- Egypt and Mesopotamia traded in grain; Rome minted coins and used salt.
- Pacific islands used Rai stones, and Aztecs used cocoa beans.

Key Idea: Money changes with culture and need, but the goal remains—easy and fair exchange.

Check Yourself

MCQs

1. What was used as money in ancient China before coins?
a) Cloth
b) Cowrie shells
c) Beads

2. Which Indian coins had symbols instead of rulers' faces?
a) Roman coins
b) Punch-marked coins
c) Rai stones

Short Answer
Q: Why do you think Rai stones were used even though they were too heavy to carry?

Creative Question
Design your own ancient currency for your tribe. What will you use and why?

Beyond the Book

Project Suggestion:
Make an "Ancient Money Museum" corner in class. Use clay, shells, paper, and foil to make replicas of:

- Punch-marked coins
- Chinese knife coins
- Cocoa beans
- Beads or salt blocks

Write short description cards for each.

Chapter 4

The Indian Rupee

Our Currency Story

Real-Life Scenario

You go to a shop to buy a notebook. The shopkeeper asks for 30. You hand over a 50 note and get change. But have you ever wondered—what is this symbol? Where did the Rupee come from? Who prints it?

Let's travel through India's money history to discover the fascinating story of the Rupee.

Curiosity Question

Why is our currency called the Rupee, and who decides what it looks like?

Explore

1. What is the Rupee?

The Rupee is the official currency of India. Its symbol is , and it is

issued by the Reserve Bank of India (RBI).
1 = 100 paise

2. The Origin of the Word "Rupee"

The word Rupee comes from the Sanskrit word "Rupya", which means "wrought silver". Ancient Indian coins were often made of silver.

3. Ancient India – Where It All Began

- As early as 600 BCE, India used punch-marked silver coins.
- During the Maurya Empire, coins were standardized with marks and weights.
- In the Gupta period, gold coins called "dinars" were used.

4. Sher Shah Suri and the Silver Rupiya (1540s CE)

One of the biggest steps in India's money history came from Sher Shah Suri, who ruled parts of India in the 1500s.

- Introduced a silver coin called the "Rupiya" weighing 178 grains (~11 grams)
- This was the first time a standard currency unit was created in India
- Mughal emperors later adopted it

5. Colonial Era – Coins of the British Raj

- The British East India Company minted coins in the 1700s
- Silver Rupees with Queen Victoria's face became common
- In 1862, India had its first uniform currency system

Did You Know?

Before this, each kingdom had its own coins—many people carried different types when traveling.

6. After Independence (Post-1947)

India introduced new coins and notes:

- First banknotes in independent India were issued in 1949

- The Lion Capital of Ashoka replaced the British monarch's image
- Coins began to feature Indian culture, science, and freedom fighters

7. Decimalisation of Currency (1957)

Before 1957:

- 1 Rupee = 16 Annas = 64 Pice = 192 Paisa

Confusing, right?
To simplify, India adopted the decimal system:
1 Rupee = 100 Paise

8. The Indian Currency Symbol (2010)

In 2010, the Indian government introduced a unique symbol:

- Designed by D. Udaya Kumar
- Combines Devanagari 'र' and Latin 'R'
- Symbol of India's cultural heritage and global growth

9. Who Prints and Controls Money in India?

- Reserve Bank of India (RBI) – Issues and regulates money
- Security Printing and Minting Corporation of India (SPMCIL) – Prints banknotes and mints coins

Fun Fact: The RBI is like the "guardian" of the Rupee!

10. Features of Modern Indian Notes

Indian notes are colorful, meaningful, and secure. They have:

- Mahatma Gandhi's image
- Swachh Bharat logo
- Regional languages panel (15+ languages)
- Hidden security thread, watermark, color-changing ink

Illustration idea:

Labeled 100 note showing security features like watermark, micro lettering, color thread.

11. The New Series – "Mahatma Gandhi (New)" Notes

Since 2016, RBI has introduced new designs:

- 10 to 2000 notes
- Show Indian heritage: Sun Temple, Rani ki Vav, Mangalyaan, Ellora Caves
- Vibrant colors and smaller sizes

Try It

Activity 1: Design Your Own Currency Note

Create a currency note for India. Include:

- A freedom fighter or national symbol
- A security feature
- A slogan for the nation

Activity 2: Rupee Timeline

Draw a timeline from:

- Punch-marked coins → Sher Shah's Rupiya → British coins → Post-independence → Decimalisation → Symbol → Gandhi New Series

Paste pictures or draw each stage!

Think & Reflect

1. Why is having a national currency important?
2. What does the design of a currency note say about a country?
3. Should India add more regional languages or heroes to its currency? Why?

Let's Revise

Quick Recap:

- The Indian Rupee comes from the Sanskrit word "Rupya" (silver).
- Sher Shah Suri introduced the first standardized Rupiya coin.
- India adopted decimal currency in 1957.
- RBI controls money printing and coin minting.
- Today's Rupee notes show our culture, science, and history.

Memory Tip:

From silver coins to the symbol, the Rupee has a story of pride and progress!

Check Yourself

MCQs

1. Who introduced the silver Rupiya in India?

a) Akbar
b) Sher Shah Suri
c) Mahatma Gandhi

2. What is the value of 1 Rupee today?

a) 10 Paise
b) 100 Paise
c) 1,000 Paise

Short Answer

Q: What are two features found on modern Indian banknotes?

Creative Question

If you had to choose one monument to print on 500 note, which one would you pick and why?

Beyond the Book

Project Suggestion:
Create a "Museum of Indian Money" display in your class.

Include:

- Old coins (real or paper cutouts)
- Photos of banknotes across time
- Descriptions of milestones like decimalisation and note redesign

Chapter 5

Famous World Currencies

Real-Life Scenario
Arya's cousin lives in the USA and sends her a gift of 10 dollars.

Arya wonders: "How much is this in rupees?" She learns that every country has its own currency, and each has a unique value, symbol, and history.
Let's take a tour of the world's most famous currencies!

Curiosity Question
Why do different countries use different currencies, and what makes them valuable?

Explore

1. What is a Currency?

A currency is the official money of a country.
Each currency:

- Has its own name (like Dollar or Euro)

- Has a symbol (like $, €, ¥)
- Has a certain value compared to other currencies

Example: 1 US Dollar = ~83 (subject to change)

2. US Dollar ($)

- **Country:** United States of America
- **Symbol:** $
- **Code:** USD
- **Used in:** Over 10 countries including Ecuador, El Salvador
- **Fun Fact:** Known as the world's reserve currency, used in global trade
- Features presidents like George Washington and Abraham Lincoln
- Green in color, often called "greenbacks"

3. Euro (€)

- **Countries:** 20 countries in the European Union
- **Symbol:** €
- **Code:** EUR
- **Fun Fact:** Launched in 1999 to make trade easier in Europe
- Euro notes have images of bridges, gates, and windows – symbols of openness

4. British Pound Sterling (£)

- **Country:** United Kingdom
- **Symbol:** £
- **Code:** GBP
- One of the oldest currencies in use
- Features British monarchs and national heroes
- **Fun fact:** 1 pound is made up of 100 pence

5. Japanese Yen (¥)

- **Country:** Japan
- **Symbol:** ¥
- **Code:** JPY
- One of the most traded currencies in the world

- Coins include a hole in the center
- Notes feature scientists, poets, and Mount Fuji

6. Chinese Yuan or Renminbi (¥ / RMB)
- **Country:** China
- **Symbol:** ¥
- **Code:** CNY or RMB
- "Renminbi" means "People's Money"
- Features Mao Zedong and famous landmarks
- Increasingly used in international trade

7. Swiss Franc (CHF)
- **Country:** Switzerland
- **Symbol:** CHF
- Known for its stability and low inflation
- Notes feature artists, scientists, and multi-lingual text

8. Russian Ruble
- **Country:** Russia
- **Symbol:**
- **Code:** RUB
- Coins and notes show architecture, war memorials, and animals

9. Other Interesting Currencies
- Brazilian Real (R$) – Features Amazon animals
- Canadian Dollar (C$) – Has colorful notes and wildlife
- Australian Dollar (A$) – Notes are waterproof and plastic!

10. How Are Currency Values Compared?

Currencies are exchanged using an exchange rate.

Example:

If 1 USD = 83, then 10 USD = 830

Exchange rates change daily based on trade, economy, and demand

Try It

Activity 1: Currency Match Game

Make flashcards with currency names and countries. Shuffle and match:

- Dollar – USA
- Euro – EU
- Yen – Japan
- Rupee – India
- Pound – UK

Activity 2: International Wallet
Create a pretend travel wallet.
Include:

- 100 note
- $10 bill
- €5 note
- ¥1,000 note

Paste or draw them and write what you could buy with each.

Think & Reflect

1. Why do countries have different currencies?
2. What do you think would happen if the whole world used the same currency?
3. Which world currency do you find most interesting and why?

Let's Revise

Quick Recap:

- Every country uses a different currency.
- Famous ones include Dollar, Euro, Yen, Pound, and Yuan.
- Currencies have symbols, codes, and exchange rates.
- Money tells us about a country's history, economy, and culture.

Memory Tip:
$ € £ ¥ – Different signs, one goal: to help people trade!

Check Yourself

MCQs

1. What is the currency of the European Union?
a) Pound
b) Dollar
c) Euro

2. Which currency is symbolized by ¥?
a) Swiss Franc
b) Japanese Yen
c) Russian Ruble

Short Answer
Q: What does "exchange rate" mean?

Creative Question
Design a new world currency. What would you name it? What would it show? Who would use it?

Beyond the Book

Project Suggestion:
Create a currency passport! Choose 5 world currencies.
Include:
- Currency name & symbol
- Image of a note/coin
- Famous figure or feature
- Current exchange rate with INR

Display it like a real passport!

Chapter 6

Central Banks

Who Controls the Money?

Real-Life Scenario

You go to the market and find that your favorite chocolate bar now costs 60 instead of 50. Your parents say, "Inflation is rising!" But who decides how much money should be printed or how inflation is controlled?

That's the job of a Central Bank. Let's find out what it does!

Curiosity Question

Who decides how much money is enough, and who keeps a check on it?

Explore

1. What Is a Central Bank?

A central bank is the main financial institution in a country that:

- Prints and issues currency
- Manages inflation and interest rates

- Keeps the banking system stable
- Helps the government in financial planning

It is like the "headteacher" of all other banks!

2. The Reserve Bank of India (RBI)

In India, the central bank is called the Reserve Bank of India.

- **Established:** April 1, 1935
- **Headquarters:** Mumbai
- **Governor:** The chief of RBI (appointed by the government)
- **Motto:** "Seva meva jayate" (Service above all)

The RBI is the only institution allowed to print currency notes in India.

3. Key Functions of a Central Bank

Issuing Currency

- RBI designs and prints notes
- It makes sure there's not too much or too little money

Controlling Inflation

- Inflation = Prices going up too fast
- RBI controls inflation by changing interest rates
- Lower interest rates = more spending
- Higher rates = less spending

Managing Other Banks

- RBI is the "bank of banks"
- It gives guidelines to commercial banks like SBI, HDFC, etc.
- Ensures they follow rules and keep people's money safe

Managing Foreign Exchange

- RBI manages how rupees are exchanged for dollars, euros, etc.
- Keeps the exchange rate stable

Government Banker

- RBI helps the government borrow or manage national funds
- Issues bonds and treasury bills

4. Why Can't We Just Print More Money?

A common question: "Why doesn't the government print lots of money and give it to everyone?"

Here's why:

- Too much money = more demand for goods
- But supply stays the same → prices go up
- That's inflation

Real wealth is in what a country produces, not how much money it prints

5. Other Famous Central Banks Around the World

Country	Central Bank Name	Currency
USA	Federal Reserve (Fed)	Dollar ($)
UK	Bank of England	Pound (£)
EU	European Central Bank (ECB)	Euro (€)
Japan	Bank of Japan	Yen (¥)
China	People's Bank of China	Yuan (¥)

All these banks play similar roles to RBI in their countries.

6. RBI's Role in a Crisis

During economic crises (like COVID-19), RBI:

- Reduced interest rates to support people and businesses
- Gave more money to banks to lend to others
- Helped stabilize the economy

7. RBI and Digital India

RBI supports:

- UPI (Unified Payments Interface)
- Digital Rupee pilot project
- Online banking security guidelines

The RBI is guiding India into a cashless, digital future while keeping things safe.

Try It

Activity 1: RBI Governor for a Day
Imagine you are the RBI Governor. What steps will you take if prices of essential items like food or fuel suddenly go up?

Activity 2: Role Play – The Money Chain

Form groups:

- One group acts as the RBI
- One group as commercial banks
- One group as customers

Act out how money moves from RBI → banks → people, and how loans and interest work.

Think & Reflect

1. Why do you think we need a central bank?
2. What would happen if banks were not regulated?
3. Is it a good idea to allow anyone to print money? Why or why not?

Let's Revise

Quick Recap:

- A central bank manages a country's money and banking system.
- In India, this is the RBI.
- It controls inflation, prints currency, manages other banks, and keeps money safe.
- Central banks exist in every major country.
- They help maintain stability during crises and support digital payment systems.

Memory Tip:
RBI = Rules, Banking, Inflation

Check Yourself

MCQs

1. What is the name of India's central bank?
a) SBI
b) RBI
c) HDFC

2. What does the RBI do when inflation rises too fast?
a) Prints more money
b) Reduces interest rates
c) Increases interest rates

Short Answer
Q: Why can't governments just print unlimited money?

Creative Question
Design a poster showing the duties of a central bank using drawings and keywords.

Beyond the Book

Project Suggestion:

Create a model "Bank of Class 6" with:

- A student as RBI Governor
- A student team as commercial bankers
- Fake currency for transactions
- Record deposits, loans, and interest

Hold a "Bank Day" where the class runs the system for 1 hour!

Chapter 7

Exchange Rates

Why Currencies Change Value

Story Starter
Aarav's uncle sends him 10 US dollars from America. Aarav goes online to check how much it is in Indian Rupees. Last week, 1 dollar was 82. Today, it's 83!

Why did it change? Who decides this? That's what we call the exchange rate—and it moves all the time!

Curiosity Question
Why does 1 dollar not always equal the same number of rupees?

Explore

1. What is an Exchange Rate?

An exchange rate tells us how much one country's currency is worth compared to another's.

Example:
If 1 USD = 83, then with 10 USD, you'll get 830.

2. How Are Exchange Rates Set?

Exchange rates change every day.

They are affected by:

- **Demand and Supply:** If many people want US dollars, its value increases.
- **Imports and Exports:** Countries that sell more goods get stronger currencies.
- **Interest Rates:** Higher interest rates attract investors, increasing currency value.
- **Inflation:** Higher inflation reduces the currency's value.
- **News and Events:** Wars, elections, or natural disasters affect currency confidence.

3. Fixed vs Floating Exchange Rate

Type	Meaning	Example
Fixed	Government decides the rate	Chinese Yuan (CNY)
Floating	Based on market demand and supply	Indian Rupee (INR), US Dollar (USD)

India follows a managed float—a mix of both.

4. Why Do Exchange Rates Matter?

International Trade

If rupee becomes weaker, imported goods (like oil, phones) cost more.
If rupee becomes stronger, we can buy more from other countries.

Travel Abroad

Planning to visit Japan or Europe? A strong rupee helps you spend more. A weak rupee means you'll need more money for the same things.

Studying Overseas
Exchange rate affects how much it costs to pay for education in dollars or euros.

Sending Money to India
NRIs (Indians living abroad) check exchange rates to send more money to family.

5. What Is Currency Appreciation and Depreciation?
Appreciation: Currency becomes stronger
Example: 1 USD = 80 (last week 83) → Rupee appreciated

Depreciation: Currency becomes weaker
Example: 1 USD = 85 (last week 83) → Rupee depreciated

Appreciation is good for importers, depreciation is good for exporters.

6. Real-Life Example: How Exchange Rate Affects You
Imagine your school orders smart boards from Germany. If the rupee is weak, they become more expensive, so your school may delay the order.

But if India exports mangoes to Europe, and the rupee is weaker, Indian mangoes become cheaper there—so farmers earn more.

7. Who Manages India's Exchange Rate?
The Reserve Bank of India (RBI):
- Keeps an eye on big ups and downs
- Buys or sells US dollars to stabilize the rupee
- Doesn't fix the rate but influences it

Try It

Activity 1: Currency Calculator Challenge

Use today's rates (or a table provided) to solve:

- Convert 1,000 into USD, EUR, and JPY
- Find how much you'd get if the rates changed tomorrow

Activity 2: News Watch

Track INR to USD rate for a week. Note the daily change. Try to guess what might have caused the change (news, events, etc.)

Think & Reflect

1. Why do you think a strong rupee helps travelers?
2. Is a weak currency always a bad thing? Why or why not?
3. How can exchange rates affect farmers or shopkeepers?

Let's Revise

Quick Recap:

- Exchange rate tells how much one currency is worth in another.
- It changes daily due to supply, demand, inflation, trade, and news.
- A stronger rupee helps importers and travelers.
- A weaker rupee helps exporters and people receiving money from abroad.
- The RBI helps keep exchange rates stable.

Memory Tip:

If the rupee goes up, imports are cheap.
If the rupee goes down, exports go deep!

Check Yourself

MCQs

1. What does "currency depreciation" mean?
a) Currency becomes stronger
b) Currency becomes weaker
c) Price of goods fall

2. Who helps manage India's exchange rate?
a) SBI
b) IMF
c) RBI

Short Answer
Q: How does the exchange rate affect someone studying abroad?

Creative Question
Imagine you run an import-export business. The rupee just depreciated. What will you do next?

Beyond the Book

Project Suggestion

Make a "Currency Tracker" chart. For 5 days, record exchange rates of:
- USD to INR
- EUR to INR
- JPY to INR

Write one sentence each day about how the rupee changed.

Chapter 8

Digital Money

UPI, e-Wallets & Cryptocurrencies

Story Starter
Arjun and his mother are buying vegetables at a roadside stall. When it's time to pay, his mother doesn't take out her wallet. She just scans a QR code using her phone and says, "Done!"

"No cash?" asks Arjun. "Nope," she smiles. "Just digital money."

Curiosity Question
How can money exist without coins or notes? Is it safe?

Explore

1. What Is Digital Money?

Digital money is money stored and used electronically. You don't need coins or paper to use it.

It can be:

- In a bank account
- Inside a mobile app
- On a digital wallet or card

You can't touch it, but it works just like real money!

2. What Is UPI? (Unified Payments Interface)

- UPI is an Indian payment system that lets you send or receive money instantly using a phone.
- Developed by NPCI (National Payments Corporation of India)
- **You can pay using:**
  - o QR codes
  - o Mobile numbers
  - o UPI IDs (like name@bank)

Examples: PhonePe, Google Pay, Paytm, BHIM

Fun Fact: India is one of the world leaders in digital payments because of UPI!

3. What Are e-Wallets?

An e-Wallet is like a digital purse on your phone.

You can:

- Add money from your bank account
- Use it to pay bills, shop online, or buy tickets
- Track your spending

Examples: Paytm Wallet, Amazon Pay, Mobikwik

4. Debit Cards vs Credit Cards

- **Debit Card:** Uses money you already have
- **Credit Card:** Lets you borrow money and pay later
- Both are swiped or tapped at shops and online

Security Features: PINs, OTPs, and biometric locks help keep your digital money safe.

5. Digital Rupee – India's Own Digital Currency

In 2023, RBI started testing the Digital Rupee (e) – India's official digital currency.

- Just like a note, but used on mobile
- Backed by RBI, so it's safe
- Helps reduce cost of printing notes

6. What Are Cryptocurrencies?

A cryptocurrency is digital money that is not controlled by any government.

Examples:

- Bitcoin (BTC)
- Ethereum (ETH)
- Dogecoin (DOGE)

Uses blockchain technology to keep transactions secure and transparent.

Warning: Cryptocurrencies are very risky. In India, they are not legal tender but allowed for private use with caution.

7. Advantages of Digital Money

- Instant Payments
- Easy to carry
- No need for change
- Better record keeping
- Contactless during pandemics

8. Risks and Precautions

- Hackers can steal passwords
- Fake QR codes
- Too much screen time = impulsive spending

Safety Tips:

- Never share PINs or OTPs
- Double-check QR codes
- Use trusted apps only
- Talk to parents before trying a new app

9. India's Digital Future

India is leading the world in financial inclusion—bringing digital payments even to rural areas.

From chaiwalas to supermarkets, digital money is everywhere!

Government Initiatives:

- Jan Dhan Yojana: Bank accounts for all
- DigiLocker and Aadhaar-linked payments
- Digital India campaign

Try It

Activity 1: Cash vs Digital Debate

Split the class into two teams:

- **Team A:** Cash is better
- **Team B:** Digital is better

Each gives reasons and examples!

Activity 2: Make a Mock QR Code

Design your own QR code (paper version). Add your name, pretend phone number, and amount. Practice "scanning" and "paying" in groups!

Think & Reflect

1. Is it okay to go 100% cashless?
2. What happens if your phone battery dies and you have no cash?

3. What would you like to see in India's Digital Rupee?

Let's Revise

Quick Recap:

- Digital money is used via phones or cards
- UPI and e-Wallets make daily payments easy
- Digital Rupee is India's official virtual currency
- Cryptocurrencies are decentralized and risky
- Stay safe by protecting passwords and using trusted apps

Memory Tip:

Swipe, scan, tap – digital money's a snap!

Check Yourself

MCQs

1. What does UPI stand for?

a) Universal Payment Idea
b) Unified Payments Interface
c) Unique Personal Income

2. Which of these is a cryptocurrency?

a) Paytm
b) Bitcoin
c) UPI

Short Answer

Q: Name two differences between e-Wallets and credit cards.

Creative Question

Design your own safe and fun digital payment app for kids. What will it be called? How will it work?

Beyond the Book

Project Suggestion
Interview a shopkeeper or vendor who uses UPI.

Ask:

- Why they prefer digital money
- What problems they've faced
- How customers react

Present your findings in class as a poster or slideshow.

Chapter 9

Inflation, Deflation & the Cost of Living

Story Starter
Ria's grandfather says, "In my time, a plate of samosas cost just 2." Ria laughs—she pays 30 now! "That's called inflation," her father explains.

Things didn't get bigger—but money became smaller in value.

Curiosity Question
Why do prices keep rising, and what does it mean for our money?

Explore

1. What is Inflation?
Inflation means the general increase in prices over time.

Example: If a pen costs 10 today and 12 next year, there's inflation.

Inflation reduces the purchasing power of money. You can buy less with the same amount.

2. What Causes Inflation?

More Demand, Same Supply
When many people want something, but it's in short supply → prices go up.

Increased Cost of Making Things
If fuel, raw materials, or wages increase → final products become costlier.

Too Much Money in the Economy
If people have more money but goods are limited → demand rises → prices rise

3. What Is Deflation?

Deflation is the opposite of inflation: prices go down over time. Sounds good? Not really.

Deflation can:

- Reduce profits for businesses
- Cause job cuts
- Slow down the economy

4. How Is Inflation Measured?

India uses a tool called the Consumer Price Index (CPI).

- It tracks prices of daily items like food, fuel, clothes, etc.
- If CPI goes up, inflation is rising

Example: If CPI was 100 last year and 106 now → 6% inflation

5. Who Controls Inflation in India?

The Reserve Bank of India (RBI):

- Monitors inflation through interest rates
- Raises rates to slow spending (fight inflation)
- Lowers rates to boost spending (fight deflation)

6. What Is "Cost of Living"?
It means how much money you need to live comfortably.

Includes:
- Food and groceries
- Rent or housing
- Transportation
- School fees and health

Cities like Mumbai or Delhi have higher cost of living than small towns.

7. Real-Life Effects of Inflation
- **For Families:** Grocery bills rise
- **For Schools:** Fees and books cost more
- **For Workers:** Salaries must increase to match rising prices
- **For Savings:** 1,000 today will buy less next year

Fun Tip: If prices rise 6% a year, in 10 years they almost double!

8. Good vs Bad Inflation
- Mild Inflation (2–6%) is okay
  - o Encourages people to spend
  - o Keeps economy active

- High Inflation (above 8%) is harmful
  - o Makes things expensive
  - o Hurts poor and fixed income groups

9. Hyperinflation – When Money Breaks
Hyperinflation = Extremely rapid price rise

Example:
Zimbabwe (2008) – prices doubled every day
A loaf of bread cost millions of dollars!

People used wheelbarrows full of cash to buy groceries!

Try It

Activity 1: Price Then vs Now
Ask grandparents or parents how much common items (milk, bus fare, movie ticket) cost 20 years ago. Compare with today's prices and make a chart.

Activity 2: Class Budget Planning
Your class receives 1,000 monthly to spend on games, books, and snacks.

- Make a budget
- Now increase item prices by 10% (simulate inflation)
- Adjust the plan

Think & Reflect

1. How does inflation affect your pocket money?
2. Can prices go down too much? What happens then?
3. Is it better to save or spend in times of inflation?

Let's Revise

Quick Recap:

- Inflation means rising prices; deflation means falling prices.
- Measured using CPI in India.
- RBI controls inflation using interest rates.
- Inflation reduces the value of money over time.
- A small amount of inflation is good. Too much is bad.

Memory Tip:
Inflation makes things cost more…
So save and spend smart, to avoid being poor!

Check Yourself

MCQs

1. What is used to measure inflation in India?
a) RBI
b) CPI
c) ATM

2. What is deflation?
a) Prices going up
b) Prices staying same
c) Prices going down

Short Answer
Q: What are two problems caused by high inflation?

Creative Question
Design a comic strip showing how a chocolate bar's price changes over 10 years due to inflation.

Beyond the Book

Project Suggestion
Create a "Classroom Price Index".
Track 5 items sold in the school canteen for a month.
Note any changes in price and make your own inflation chart.

Chapter 10

Counterfeit Money

How to Spot Fakes

Story Starter

Tanvi's uncle runs a shop. One day, someone gives him a 500 note. It looks real, but later the bank says it's fake. He loses 500!
Tanvi asks, "But how can we know if money is real or not?"
Let's learn the tricks that keep our money safe and smart.

Curiosity Question

How can you tell the difference between real and fake money?

Explore

1. What Is Counterfeit Money?

Counterfeit money is fake money made to look real.

- Criminals print fake notes to trick people
- It's illegal and harms the economy
- It's like cheating the whole country!

2. Why Is Counterfeit Money Dangerous?

It causes:

- Loss to honest people and businesses
- Trouble for banks and RBI
- Lower trust in money
- Can be linked to crime or terrorism

3. How Does India Fight Fake Notes?

The Reserve Bank of India (RBI) adds security features to currency so you can spot fakes easily.

4. Features of Real Indian Notes

Let's look at a real 500 note:

Watermark

Hold the note against light. You'll see:

- Mahatma Gandhi's image
- The numeral "500"

Security Thread

A silver strip that changes color from green to blue

See-through Register

The number "500" perfectly lines up when held to light

Micro-lettering

Tiny text "RBI" and "500" near Gandhi's image

Color-Changing Ink

The number "500" changes color when tilted

Raised Printing

Feel the roughness on:

- Mahatma Gandhi's glasses

- RBI seal
- Ashoka pillar

Identification Mark (for visually challenged)
A circle, triangle or diamond that you can feel

Language Panel
Shows denomination in 15 Indian languages

Swachh Bharat Logo
Symbol of cleanliness and national pride

Illustration idea:
A labeled diagram of a 500 note showing all key security features

5. Common Tricks Used in Fakes

- No watermark
- Blurry images
- Wrong size or paper
- Missing micro-text
- Dull colors or wrong font

Always compare with a note from an ATM or bank if unsure!

6. What Should You Do If You Find a Fake Note?

- Don't try to use it
- Give it to your nearest bank branch or police station
- RBI will check it and report it

Never share fake notes—even by mistake. It's against the law.

7. Tech vs Fakes

RBI is using:

- Plastic/polymer notes (coming soon)

• Digital rupee (can't be faked)
• Smart machines to detect fake notes

The more digital India becomes, the less chance of fake money

8. Fake Currency Around the World
• In the US, fake dollars are a serious issue
• In Europe, fake euros are tracked closely by the European Central Bank
• Some countries use plastic notes to stop copying

Try It

Activity 1: Note Check Challenge
Bring a clean 100, 200, or 500 note (or photo).
Use a checklist to find all security features.

Mark for each found!

Activity 2: Design a Safe Currency

Create your own note with at least 5 security features:
• Watermark
• Secret code
• Color shift
• Raised pattern
• Personal logo

Think & Reflect

1. Why is fake currency a danger to honest people?
2. Do you think digital money is safer? Why?
3. What more can be done to stop counterfeit money?

Let's Revise

Quick Recap:

- Counterfeit money is fake currency made illegally
- It causes financial loss and national harm
- RBI adds security features like watermark, thread, micro-lettering
- You can spot fakes with care and knowledge
- If you get a fake note, report it—never reuse it

Memory Tip:
Feel, look, tilt—and you'll know if it's real!

Check Yourself

MCQs

1. What does a watermark show on a 500 note?
a) A barcode
b) A hidden image of Mahatma Gandhi
c) The Ashoka Pillar

2. What should you do with a fake note?
a) Spend it quickly
b) Tear it up
c) Report it to a bank or police

Short Answer
Q: Name three features you can use to check if a note is real.

Creative Question
Invent a futuristic anti-fake technology for notes. How would it work?

Beyond the Book

Project Suggestion

Create a poster titled "7 Ways to Spot a Fake Note." Use real-life images or sketches of Indian currency. Hang it in your classroom or school library.

Chapter 11

Designing a Currency

Symbols, People & Stories

Story Starter
Rehan looks closely at a 100 note. He sees Mahatma Gandhi, a clean India symbol, and the beautiful Rani ki Vav stepwell. "Why are these pictures here?" he wonders.
Great question, Rehan! Let's explore how every currency tells a story.

Curiosity Question
What do the pictures, colors, and symbols on money say about a country?

Explore

1. Currency: A Country's Calling Card

Money isn't just for spending—it shows the world what a country is proud of.

Designs can include:

- National leaders
- Cultural landmarks
- Important animals, events, or values

Money = Mini-story of your nation's identity!

2. Who Designs Currency in India?

- The Reserve Bank of India (RBI) and the Ministry of Finance
- Artists, historians, and designers work together
- Final design includes both beauty and security features

3. What You See on Indian Banknotes

Mahatma Gandhi

- Appears on all modern Indian notes
- Symbol of peace, unity, and freedom

Swachh Bharat Logo

- On every new note to remind people about cleanliness

Heritage Sites & Scientific Achievements

Part of the Mahatma Gandhi (New) Series:

Note	Design on Back
10	Sun Temple, Konark
20	Ellora Caves
50	Hampi with Chariot
100	Rani ki Vav (stepwell)
200	Sanchi Stupa
500	Red Fort
2000	Mangalyaan (India's Mars mission)

Languages Panel
Shows the denomination in 15 Indian languages + Hindi and English

4. What About Coins?

Coins show:

- The Lion Capital of Ashoka
- Symbols for visually challenged (dot, bar, triangle)
- Emblems like Parliament House, agriculture, and technology

Fun Fact: India's 5 and 10 coins have been redesigned for better grip and clarity!

5. Colors & Size

Each note is a different color and size to help people identify them easily.

- Bright colors
- Bigger denominations = larger notes
- Consistent fonts and shapes

6. Global Examples of Currency Design

US Dollar

- Features former presidents (George Washington, Abraham Lincoln)
- Green color, minimal changes

British Pound

- Shows Queen Elizabeth II or King Charles III
- Famous scientists like Newton

Canadian Dollar

- Colorful notes
- Wildlife like loons, polar bears
- Uses polymer to avoid damage

Japanese Yen
- Elegant portraits of poets and scientists
- Traditional art scenes

7. Why Design Matters

Good design helps:
- Prevent fakes
- Represent culture
- Make usage easier for all, including the visually impaired

Currency = Art + Security + Pride

8. Should Kids Help Design Money?

Absolutely! Imagine if kids voted for:
- A national hero
- A freedom fighter
- A famous invention
- A local language quote

Designing money helps kids learn history, civics, and responsibility.

Try It

Activity 1: Create Your Own Currency Note

Draw a 100 or 2000 note. Include:
- National symbol
- A person you admire
- Your favorite Indian monument
- A safety feature (watermark, thread, etc.)

Activity 2: Gallery Walk

Display everyone's notes in class. Vote on:
- Most meaningful design
- Most creative safety feature
- Best color scheme

Think & Reflect

1. Why is Mahatma Gandhi on all our notes?
2. Which monument or person would you like to see on a note and why?
3. What can currency designs teach us about our history and values?

Let's Revise

Quick Recap:
- Currency designs reflect national identity and cultural pride
- India's notes show Mahatma Gandhi, heritage sites, and clean India mission
- Different countries honor their leaders, nature, or values
- Coins and notes are also designed to help the visually challenged
- Designing money is a mix of security, beauty, and meaning

Memory Tip:
Money is not just math—it's a museum in your pocket!

Check Yourself

MCQs

1. What does the 100 note in the new series show?
a) India Gate
b) Rani ki Vav
c) Taj Mahal

2. What symbol appears on all Indian coins?
a) Lotus

b) Parliament
c) Lion Capital of Ashoka

Short Answer
Q: Name three things commonly found on Indian banknotes.

Creative Question
If you were to design a 1,000 note for the future, what message would you want it to send?

Beyond the Book

Project Suggestion
Hold a "Currency Design Day."
Students design notes for a future India.
Include themes like climate action, equality, space science, or culture.
Create a digital gallery and share it with parents or school visitors.

Chapter 12

Currency and You

Budgeting, Saving & Earning

Story Starter
Manya receives 200 as her monthly pocket money. She wants to buy storybooks, play a game at the arcade, and save for her friend's birthday gift. But she can't do all of it!
She thinks, "How can I use my money smartly?"
That's where budgeting and saving come in.

Curiosity Question
What is the best way to manage the money you have?

Explore

1. What Is Personal Finance?
Personal finance means how you manage your own money.
It includes:
- Earning

- Spending
- Saving
- Budgeting
- Planning for the future

Even as students, learning to handle money helps you become smart and independent.

2. What Is a Budget?
A budget is a plan for how you will spend and save your money.

Formula:
Income – Expenses = Savings
If you earn 500 and spend 400 → you save 100

3. Income: Where Does Money Come From?

For children:
- Pocket money
- Gifts on birthdays/festivals
- Rewards for chores or achievements

For adults:
- Salary
- Business profit
- Pension
- Investments

Earning is the first step in handling money—but not the only one.

4. Expenses: Where Does Money Go?
Money is spent on:
- **Needs:** food, school supplies, travel
- **Wants:** toys, snacks, games
- **Giving:** charity, gifts

Smart tip: First spend on needs, then save, and only then buy wants.

5. Saving: Why It's Important

Saving helps you:

- Handle emergencies
- Buy something special later
- Build habits of discipline

Goal Saving: Saving for a purpose (like a bicycle or a school trip)
Start with a piggy bank, move to a bank account when older.

6. Smart Spending: Ask Before You Buy

Before you spend, ask:

- Do I really need this?
- Is there a better option?
- Can I wait for a discount?
- Will I still want this after 3 days?

This is called being a mindful consumer.

7. Growing Your Money: Simple Interest

Some savings can grow over time!

Example:

You save 1,000 in a bank at 5% interest.
After 1 year, you get 1,050.
This is called interest—extra money earned by saving.

8. The 50-30-20 Rule (Simple Budgeting for Kids)

Use	% of Your Money
Needs (must-haves)	50%
Wants (fun things)	30%
Savings	20%

If you get 500:
250 on needs, 150 on wants, 100 saved

9. Earning Ideas for Students

At your age, earning is more about learning responsibility:
- Selling old books or crafts at a school fair
- Helping in a family shop
- Winning contests with prize money
- Doing chores for rewards

Earning teaches effort = reward

10. Digital Banking for Teens

Today, banks offer:
- Junior accounts (with parent permission)
- Prepaid cards
- Saving apps

Start early and learn digital responsibility:
- Set limits
- Track spending
- Avoid scams

Try It

Activity 1: Pocket Money Planner

Make a table for one month:

- Income (pocket money, gifts)
- Expenses (books, snacks)
- Savings (piggy bank)

Review at month's end: How well did you do?

Activity 2: Savings Challenge

Set a goal: e.g., save 200 in 4 weeks

- Skip 1 treat a week
- Earn by doing extra chores
- Track and celebrate your goal!

Think & Reflect

1. Why is saving important even if you don't earn much?
2. Can spending too much on fun stop you from reaching your goals?
3. How can you make your own mini-budget each month?

Let's Revise

Quick Recap:

- Personal finance is about how you earn, spend, save, and grow money
- A budget helps you control money, not the other way around
- Start saving now to build a better future
- Learn to spend wisely and track your expenses
- Smart money habits start young!

Memory Tip:
Earn with effort. Save with care. Spend with thought. Grow v
time.

Check Yourself

MCQs

1. What is a budget?
a) A shopping list
b) A money-spending app
c) A plan for income and expenses

2. Which of these is a "need"?
a) School notebook
b) Video game
c) Ice cream

Short Answer
Q: Name two ways kids can earn money or rewards respons

Creative Question
Design a poster that teaches kids: "How to Be Smart with M

Beyond the Book

Project Suggestion
Create a "Money Journal" for 2 weeks:
- Note your earnings, spendings, and savings daily
- Write one money lesson you learn each day
- Share with the class at the end!